CHOOSING 360

A GUIDE TO EVALUATING
MULTI-RATER FEEDBACK INSTRUMENTS
FOR MANAGEMENT DEVELOPMENT

CHOOSING 360

A GUIDE TO EVALUATING
MULTI-RATER FEEDBACK INSTRUMENTS
FOR MANAGEMENT DEVELOPMENT

Ellen Van Velsor
Jean Brittain Leslie
John W. Fleenor

Center for Creative Leadership
Greensboro, North Carolina

The Center for Creative Leadership is an international, nonprofit educational institution founded in 1970 to advance the understanding, practice, and development of leadership for the benefit of society worldwide. As a part of this mission, it publishes books and reports that aim to contribute to a general process of inquiry and understanding in which ideas related to leadership are raised, exchanged, and evaluated. The ideas presented in its publications are those of the author or authors.

The Center thanks you for supporting its work through the purchase of this volume. If you have comments, suggestions, or questions about any Center publication, please contact John R. Alexander, President, at the address given below.

Center for Creative Leadership
Post Office Box 26300
Greensboro, North Carolina 27438-6300

Center for
Creative Leadership
leadership. learning. life.

CCL No. 334

Library of Congress Cataloging-in-Publication Data

Van Velsor, Ellen
    Choosing 360 : a guide to evaluating multi-rater feedback instruments for management development / Ellen Van Velsor, Jean Brittain Leslie, John W. Fleenor.
        p. cm.
    Update ed. of: Feedback to managers, vol. 1. 1991.
    Includes bibliographical references (p.   ).
    ISBN 1-882197-30-5
    1. Organizational effectiveness—Evaluation—Methodology. 2. Feedback (Psychology). 3. Executives—Rating of. I. Leslie, Jean Brittain. II. Fleenor, John W. III. Morrison, Ann M. Feedback to managers. IV. Title.
    HD58.9.V36 1997
    658.4'03—dc21   97-18853
                                                                         CIP

Table of Contents

Foreword

At the end of 1991, CCL published the two-volume *Feedback to Managers (Volume I: A Guide to Evaluating Multi-rater Feedback Instruments; Volume II: A Review and Comparison of Sixteen Multi-rater Feedback Instruments)*. Since that time, there has been a notable increase of interest in multi-rater, or 360-degree, instruments: More are available; they are being used for a wider range of purposes; and much has been learned about their use. A revision is thus in order. What you will find here is an updated edition of the first volume (with a new edition of the second currently in progress).

The text has been thoroughly reviewed by the authors—Ellen Van Velsor and Jean Brittain Leslie, who wrote the original edition, and John Fleenor, who joined the team for this version—and changes have been made to reflect current understandings in the field—for instance, new information on the proper use of norms and on "item banks" (a collection of instrument items that have been tested for reliability and validity) has been added, and the section on validity has been redone.

You will note that this work has been retitled and that it is no longer referred to as the first volume of a set. We wanted to make this guide, which can help practitioners begin to make sense of the complexity and proliferation of instruments, as visible as possible. The update of the second volume, also to be a stand-alone publication, will aid practitioners by providing in-depth descriptions of selected instruments, including some that were not included in the previous edition, and discussion of key issues in their use. The two can still, of course, be used together, and we invite people to do so.

Walter W. Tornow
Vice President, Research and Publication

Acknowledgments

We would like to express our appreciation to the many reviewers whose comments, ideas, and criticisms greatly improved the quality of this manuscript. These include David DeVries, Janet Spence, Russ Moxley, Michael Hoppe, Maxine Dalton, Lloyd Bond, and members of the Center for Creative Leadership's Writers' Group. We are also indebted to Clark Wilson, Walt Tornow, David Campbell, and Philip Benson for several ideas presented here.

Introduction

Many organizations are using 360-degree-feedback instruments to help their managers become better leaders. These instruments are designed to collect information from different sources (or perspectives) about a target manager's performance. The principal strength of 360-degree-feedback instruments is their use of multiple perspectives. In most cases, the different sources of information (the raters) are the supervisor (or boss), the peers, and the direct reports of the target manager, although some instruments now allow managers to use internal and/or external customers as raters.

This report presents a nontechnical, step-by-step process you can use to evaluate any 360-degree-feedback instrument intended for management or leadership development. Although we have simplified this process as much as possible, it still will require some effort on your part—but effort that will pay off in terms of your having a high-quality instrument that best meets your needs.

The steps in evaluating a 360-degree-feedback instrument are laid out here sequentially. Yet all steps are not equal in complexity or importance. We suggest that you make the most critical decisions early in the process; in this way you can save some effort by eliminating instruments that don't meet your needs in terms of content and that don't pass muster when it comes to reliability and validity.

A checklist of the steps is included, for your convenience, at the end of this report. There the reader will also find a glossary of many of the technical words used here and a list of suggested readings.

STEP 1:
FIND OUT WHAT IS AVAILABLE

The availability of 360-degree-feedback instruments is increasing at a tremendous pace. You can expect that there are as many promising instruments under development as there are good instruments for sale. So your first task should be to gain some knowledge of what is out there in order to choose the best possible sample of instruments to review.

In the short run, a good way to familiarize yourself with what is available is to search one of several guides that categorize and review instruments. *Feedback to Managers, Volume II* (Van Velsor & Leslie, 1991) is one such guide. It provides basic descriptive and technical data on 360-degree-feedback instruments available for use for management development. Other guides include *Mental Measurements Yearbook* (Conoley & Impara, 1995); *Business and Industry Testing: Current Practices and Test Reviews* (Hogan & Hogan, 1990); *Psychware Sourcebook* (Krug, 1993); and *Tests: A Comprehensive Reference for Assessment in Psychology, Education and Business* (Sweetland & Keyser, 1990). These can usually be found in the reference section of libraries. Over time, it may be useful as well to keep a file of the instrument brochures you obtain, because many of the directories are not published often enough to keep you updated on the very newest products.

Step 2:
Collect a Complete Set of Materials

When you have identified several instruments you wish to evaluate, you need to obtain five pieces of information about each of them. You cannot make an informed decision using only a copy of the instrument or a promotional brochure.

Specifically, for each instrument you wish to consider, you should obtain the following:

- A copy of the instrument itself. If the instrument has one form for the individual to rate himself or herself and a separate form for the others who will rate him or her, get both.
- A sample feedback report (a representation of what the manager will receive after the instrument is scored). You can't tell what type of feedback your managers will actually receive by looking at the instrument they will fill out. The sample could be a complete report, or it could be part of a report such as an example of the feedback display in the technical or trainer's manual. Either type will do.
- A technical manual or other publication that outlines in detail the developmental and psychometric research done on the instrument.
- Information about any supporting materials that accompany the scored feedback, such as interpretive materials, development guides, goal-planning materials, and the like.
- Information about price, scoring, and whatever certification or training may be required to purchase or use the instrument.

It is not at all unreasonable to request this quantity of information. American Psychological Association guidelines (APA, 1985) require that this information be available upon request when an instrument is offered for sale.

In addition to seeking the recommended information, you should, through all the steps that follow, look for evidence of a commitment to continuous improvement on the part of each instrument's developer. This is especially true if an instrument has been around for awhile. As we will discuss in the section on validity, research should always be in progress, because no instrument can ever be considered valid once and for all. Expect revisions in the scales over time; these are often made when additional validation studies have been completed. Expect revisions in the presentation of feedback as well; these are often made as the developer learns from the experience of those who have used an instrument. It is not uncommon for good instruments to have more than one copyright date, because even small revisions to content can cause changes in other areas, such as scale weightings or instrument norms.

Step 3:
Compare Your Intended Use to Instrument Characteristics

It is improbable that one instrument will meet the needs of all managers in an organization. Job demands differ somewhat by organizational level, and even at the same management level, skills that are needed for effectiveness may change over time. In addition, the dimensions on which managers are assessed should be in line with organizational visions for leadership. To the extent that these visions vary across organizations, it is also highly unlikely that one instrument will meet the needs of all kinds of organizations. Thus, in searching for an instrument to provide feedback to managers, a person is typically looking for one that will satisfy the needs of a particular group of managers in an organization with specific leadership or management needs.

Although nearly every 360-degree-feedback instrument has a statement of purpose describing the level of management it targets, there seems to be little relationship between management level and the domains of activity or behavior assessed. An instrument targeted toward all levels of management might not be right for middle managers in your organization because the capacities assessed are not in line with company-wide management-development goals. An instrument targeted toward higher levels might be right for your middle managers if the competencies assessed agree with your management-development goals.

More important than considering the advertised audience is discovering the norm group, if any, to which managers will be compared. By *norm group,* we mean the group of managers whose scores are stored in the vendor's database and are output as the comparison group on every individual feedback report. If the norm group is comprised of senior-level managers, whose skills are likely to be more highly developed, the scores of middle managers will probably appear worse than they would if they were compared to managers similar to themselves. Therefore, look for instruments that have been normed on a sample similar to your target managers; consider level, organization type, and demographics (for example, ethnicity and gender).

But be forewarned: The feedback instruments we are concerned with here have been developed for use in management-development efforts, either in the classroom or in individual feedback settings. These are instruments that have not been developed or tested for other purposes—such as making selection or promotion decisions.

STEP 4:
EXAMINE THE FEEDBACK SCALES

In evaluating individual instruments, you should begin by examining the scales on which feedback will be received. Are you comfortable with what it measures?

There is a detailed discussion of scales in step 6, but what you need to know at this point is that the scales are made up of several items on the instrument and represent the content or competencies on which managers will be evaluated. Each individual scale represents a slice of managerial work (for example, planning) or a single kind of competency (for example, decisiveness); as a whole the scales provide a portrait of leadership or managerial effectiveness. Using the sample feedback you have obtained, you should consider the following when looking at the scales:

- Is your organization wedded to a particular way of representing what it takes to be effective in your business or do you have a particular model underlying management-development efforts?
- Does the range of scales fit with what you see as relevant competencies for managers in your target group?
- Does the number of scales seem reasonable?
- If, in your judgment, an instrument does not have enough scales that seem relevant to your target group, or if it has too many that seem irrelevant, drop it from further consideration.

STEP 5:
FAMILIARIZE YOURSELF WITH THE
INSTRUMENT-DEVELOPMENT PROCESS

In order to know how to identify quality instruments, you must understand the basics of sound instrument development.

The development process can be seen as occurring in four stages:

- developing instrument items and feedback scales,
- assessing reliability and validity,
- designing the feedback display, and
- creating supporting materials.

At each stage different issues are being addressed.

When items and scales (fully defined in step 6 below) are being developed, the author must identify, as much as possible, the full range of behaviors or skills that he or she believes represents management or leadership competency. Another question at this stage is whether items of behavior or competency cluster in groups that are internally consistent, distinct from each other, and useful for feedback purposes.

To assess reliability, the author of an instrument must consider whether the measurement of these skills or competencies is stable in a variety of ways. To assess validity, the author must determine whether the scales really measure the dimensions they were intended to measure and whether they are related to effectiveness as a manager or leader. Because 360-degree-feedback instruments are primarily intended for individual development, the question of whether the areas assessed can be developed also must be considered.

When designing feedback, the author should try to maximize the manager's understanding of the data to enhance its impact. In creating supporting materials, the aim of the author is to help the feedback recipient gain deeper understanding of the theory or research behind the instrument and thereby enhance the ability to interpret and work with the data. Your task as an evaluator is to assess the work completed in each of these four stages and balance what you find against the needs of your target group.

STEP 6:
LEARN HOW ITEMS AND FEEDBACK SCALES WERE DEVELOPED

Instruments that assess managerial competence or leadership effectiveness are dealing with complicated phenomena. These phenomena cannot be adequately represented by a single behavior or characteristic because they are comprised of many closely related behaviors and skills. To adequately measure these complex capacities, instruments must have scales that are made up of several items.

The process of instrument development typically begins with the writing of items that represent behaviors or characteristics believed to be related to effective management or leadership.

Items can come from a variety of places. Sometimes the author refers to a theory (leadership theory, theory of managerial work, competency models) to develop specific behavioral statements or statements describing characteristics or skills. At other times researchers create descriptions of characteristics or skills based on data they have collected. Another way items can be written is by basing them on the organizational experience of the author(s). People who frequently work in training or consulting with managers may feel they can capture in a set of statements the essence of the leadership or management effectiveness they have observed.

The better instruments tend to be those that have used a combination of approaches in their development. A basis in theory provides an instrument with a set of validation strategies, while empirical research can provide data from working managers. Ultimately, the quality of the final product depends on a combination of the quality of the theory, research, and experience of the developer; his or her skill in translating theory, research, and experience into written items; and the attention paid to instrument development and feedback design. A complete evaluation on your part will reveal the level of quality at all these stages.

The nature of items can vary, regardless of their origin. Items can be phrased behaviorally (for example, "Walks around to see how our work is going"), phrased as skills or competencies (for example, "Is good at influencing the right people"), or phrased as traits or personal characteristics (for example, "Is highly motivated").

Instrument feedback is usually presented to the target manager as scores on scales (groups of items). Because scales tend to be more abstract than items (for example, "Resourcefulness"), it may be difficult for target managers to set goals for change based on this type of data. To help managers process their data, some instruments provide scores on the individual items that comprise these scales.

Feedback on behavioral items may be easiest for managers to use in setting goals for change because they are the most concrete. Behavioral changes are the easiest for co-workers to see as well. Change on this type item, however, can be the most superficial in terms of enhancing personal development. At the other extreme, feedback on characteristics such as motivation can be the most difficult to use, and change on this type item can be the hardest to observe. But change on these items may be more likely to enhance personal development. Feedback on specific skills probably falls somewhere between these two extremes: It is moderately easy to use when changes are observable and it involves some real skill development.

The items discussed above are good examples. If one receives a low score on a behavioral item such as "Walks around to see how our work is going," it will be relatively easy to change (that is, "Walk around more") but will probably lead to little in the way of personal development for that manager. If one receives a low score on a skill-based item such as "Is good at influencing the right people," it will be harder to change, because the manager will have to find out how to become better and then will need to improve. But the result can be important skill development. Finally, receiving a low score on an item such as "Is highly motivated" can be the hardest of all to change. Change will require the manager to reflect and discover why motivation is low, and to decide what it will take to feel more motivated. Then the manager will have to make whatever personal or life changes are necessary. This kind of change, however, can be the more developmental.

If individuals are left on their own to process feedback (no trainer or facilitator is available), or if an instrument is not accompanied by comprehensive interpretive and development materials, the clarity of item content is critical. The harder items are to interpret, the more difficulty managers will have in benefiting from the feedback and the more important the quantity and quality of support becomes.

Once items are created, instrument development proceeds to the task of constructing the scales on which feedback will be given. Multiple items are grouped together to represent the set of closely related skills or behaviors that make up a managerial competency (for instance, "Resourcefulness" or "Planning and Organizing"). Responses to the items on a scale should group together to form a coherent whole, internally homogeneous and distinct from other scales.

How the scale-development process is conducted is critical, because the resulting scales will form the basis of the model of leadership, management, or effective performance that you will be presenting to the manager. Your task as the evaluator is to discover whether the process of scale construction seems reasonable and complete. To determine that, you will need to look in the technical manual or in published technical reports.

There are typically two aspects of scale development: the statistical and the rational/intuitive. The statistical aspect involves using procedures such as factor analysis, cluster analysis, or item-scale correlations to group items into scales based on the degree of similarity in response patterns of the raters (for instance, people rated high on one item are also rated high on other items in that scale). The rational/intuitive aspect involves grouping items together based on the author's expectations or experience about how different skills or behaviors relate to one another. Some instruments have used one of the two processes in developing scales from items and some have used both.

Look for some evidence of statistical analysis such as factor analysis, cluster analysis, or item-scale correlations. Although it is not important that you understand the details of these statistical procedures, it is critical to realize that their goal is to reduce a large number of items to a smaller number of scales by grouping items together based on how these behaviors or characteristics are related to each other and allowing for the deletion of items that are not working.

For example, one way of determining how well the items relate to the scales being measured is by examining the relationship between the individual items that comprise each scale and the overall scale scores. High item-scale correlations indicate that the chosen items do indeed relate closely to the scales being measured. On the other hand, items with low item-scale correlations should be dropped from the scale.

Also look at whether items grouped together by the statistical techniques make sense. Because these techniques group items according to their statistical relationship, items that are conceptually unrelated may end up on the same scale. For example, "Being attentive to the personal needs of direct reports" may be empirically related to "Maintaining an orderly work space," not because these two skills are conceptually linked but because the managers used in the analysis happened to score high on both. An intuitive look at scale composition can weed out item groupings that make little sense.

On the other hand, if feedback scales appear to have been created solely by intuitive means, be aware that there is no data to show, in fact, how well the behaviors, skills, or traits actually work together to measure a more abstract construct—the question of whether these item groupings represent actual competencies among managers remains unanswered.

　　An important consideration in the development of items and scales is the issue of customization. Some instruments use an "open architecture" approach that allows items to be added on client request. These items are usually chosen from what is known as an "item bank." Although this feature is designed to meet customer needs, there is currently professional disagreement about the degree to which this practice reduces the integrity of the instrument or adds to the knowledge base about the emerging demands of leadership.

STEP 7:
FIND OUT HOW CONSISTENT SCORES TEND TO BE

　　Information for this step and the next will again be found in the technical material for the instrument. First, look for a section on "Reliability," or sections on "Test-retest Reliability," "Internal Consistency," and "Interrater Agreement."

　　Basically, reliability is consistency. There are three aspects to reliability:

- homogeneity within scales,
- agreement within rater groups, and
- stability over time.

Without evidence of reliability, we do not know whether the items and scales of an instrument are good enough to hold up even under stable conditions with similar raters. In other words, we do not know whether items that are grouped together in a scale are measuring the same competency (homogeneity within scales); we do not know whether groups of raters who bear the same relationship to a manager tend to interpret the items similarly (agreement within rater groups); and we do not know whether the meaning of items is clear enough so that a single rater will rate a manager the same way over a relatively short period of time (stability over time).

Homogeneity within Scales:
Basic Issues in Internal Consistency

　　Homogeneity within scales is called *internal consistency*. This type of reliability applies to the scales on which feedback is to be given, rather than to the individual items to which raters respond. Reliability is assessed using a statistic called the correlation coefficient, which indicates the degree of relationship between two measures. Correlation coefficients can range from

−1 (perfect negative relationship) to +1 (perfect positive relationship). A correlation of zero means there is no relationship between the two measures of interest.

Internal consistency measures are based on the average correlation among items and the number of items in the scale. Fundamentally, it asks whether all the items that make up a single scale are, in fact, measuring the same thing, as their inclusion in a single scale suggests. Managers who exhibit one of the behaviors that defines the scale should also exhibit the behaviors described by other items on that scale. If this correlation is low, either the scale contains too few items or the items have little in common.

Though several statistical procedures exist for testing internal consistency, Cronbach's alpha is the most widely used. An alpha of .7 or higher is generally considered to be acceptable. Low reliabilities are often the result of items that are not clearly written.

It should be noted here that the interpretation of reliability coefficients (how high they should be) is a subjective process. Although we provide rules of thumb for deciding whether a particular type of coefficient is high or low, there are many issues involved in making such interpretations. For example, factors such as the number of items on a scale and what skills are being measured by a scale can affect its reliability. So it's probably a good idea to compare the reliability coefficients reported for several similar instruments before deciding what level of reliability seems to be acceptable.

Agreement within Rater Groups: Basic Issues in Interrater Reliability

Agreement within rater groups is commonly called *interrater reliability*. This concept assumes that two or more direct reports, peers, or supervisors, with an adequate opportunity to observe a manager's behavior, should tend to agree on the level of performance of that manager, given reliable items and scales.

Interrater reliability does not tend to be very high for 360-degree-feedback instruments for several reasons. First, the raters are typically untrained. Trained raters may produce higher reliability by using a common evaluative framework. The people who usually complete these instruments, however, often rely on nothing more than their own perceptions, and perceptions tend to vary. Second, a group of direct reports may be managed differently by their boss. Their within-group reliability may be relatively low because the target manager actually interacts differently with each of them. Third, some behaviors may elicit higher interrater reliability than others because they are easier to observe and rate. And fourth, interrater reliability among peers may be lower to the extent that managers interface differently with different kinds of organizational peers.

Again, this type of reliability coefficient does not tend to be very high for 360-degree-feedback instruments; it should not, however, be extremely low. Look for correlation coefficients, within specific rater groups (that is, peers, direct reports), that are at least .4.

Additional Considerations

It is not uncommon to find instruments that have not been tested for interrater reliability. There is some disagreement about whether this is necessary or useful for multiple-perspective instruments, because the perspectives taken by various raters (peers, boss, direct reports) will differ according to the organizational relationship they have with the target manager. The argument is that these differences in organizational perspective will be reflected by artificially low interrater correlations.

Yet careful analysis can be, and has been, done on reliability within the different perspectives. When approached this way, there should be higher reliability within rater groups than between them. For example, a single group, say peers, should show higher within-group reliability than do peers as compared to direct reports. This approach recognizes both the desirability of reasonable reliability among raters of the same type and the reality that disagreement exists between raters of different types.

In looking at reliability within rater groups, one needs to be wary of very high correlations, because they may be an indication of raters' overall bias toward the individual (the so-called halo effect), instead of a clear reflection of the individual's performance. Therefore, as a rule of thumb, within-group reliability should not be lower than .4 or much higher than .7.

Stability over Time:
Basic Issues in Test-retest Reliability

Stability over short periods of time is called *test-retest reliability*. It is studied in relation to both items and scales. An item or scale should be stable enough to produce a similar response this week and next week, given that no significant event, such as training, has intervened. If the meaning of an item is unclear or debatable, it may produce varying responses because of this ambiguity. Low test-retest results indicate the item should be revised and retested or dropped from the scale.

Look in the technical materials for test-retest coefficients of at least .4, which is minimally adequate, with .7 to .8 quite high. This coefficient tends to be low for items on 360-degree instruments because others' perceptions of behavior or competence may be unstable. Yet it is still important that the developer has weeded out of the instrument those items with very low stability over time.

Additional Considerations

A few instrument developers argue that test-retest reliability is inappropriate for 360-degree-feedback instruments. These developers argue that the simple act of completing a questionnaire will affect responses on a retest, and that an instrument designed to stimulate change shouldn't be assessed on these criteria. Although both of these assertions may be partly true, neither negates the need to examine test-retest correlations to look at basic item and scale stability.

Responding to a set of test items may, in fact, alert respondents to dimensions of managerial effectiveness of which they had previously been unaware. As a result, respondents may rate a manager somewhat differently on the second rating opportunity, having now had time to observe the desired behavior. This may be another reason why test-retest correlations do not typically turn out higher than .6 or so for 360-degree-feedback instruments.

Adequate test-retest reliability is especially important if you expect to use an instrument before and after training or over time to measure program impact or individual change. If test-retest reliability has not been demonstrated, you cannot know whether changes in scores over time represent real changes in performance or are merely the result of instability in the instrument itself.

In order to make a meaningful statistical comparison, the appropriate way to conduct test-retest reliability studies is to compare data from two administrations of the instrument that are completed three to six weeks apart, with no intervening feedback or training. With this method, study participants probably won't remember their initial ratings when they complete the instrument for the second time.

Although completing the form may influence the way raters observe managers or influence the way managers rate themselves, managers are not likely to change significantly merely by completing the instrument. Really significant behavioral change is quite difficult to achieve, usually requiring both powerful feedback and intense follow-up.

STEP 8:
ASSESS BASIC ASPECTS OF VALIDITY—DOES THE INSTRUMENT MEASURE WHAT IT CLAIMS TO MEASURE?

The next step is to look for evidence of validity. In the instrument-development process, this is the process of reality testing. It is here that the developer begins to see whether the model holds up for real managers in real jobs.

In other words, validity is integrity. If you do not know for sure whether an instrument measures what it says it measures and you do not have evidence that scores are related to effectiveness on the job, you will not know how to interpret data from that instrument. If you have not seen evidence that managers can improve their performance, you cannot know whether the instrument's scales represent areas in which managers are able to develop themselves.

These considerations are especially important because managers typically will use the feedback to set performance goals or to try to change their behavior, and most will take what others say very seriously. Established validity is also helpful in dealing with managers who receive very negative feedback from others. These managers may, to maintain their self-respect, attack the integrity of the instrument by arguing that it assesses areas that don't make a difference or are areas over which the manager has little control.

Studying the validity of 360-degree-feedback instruments involves three separate, but related, areas. The first is determining whether the instrument actually measures what it is intended to measure. For instance, does it measure leadership rather than intelligence or power? The second is seeing whether what is measured really makes a difference. Are higher scores actually related to greater effectiveness in real organizations? The third is evaluating whether what is measured can change as a result of training, feedback, or other developmental experiences. Can the instrument's scales be shown to represent domains that are amenable to development?

Look in the technical materials for a section on validity. There may be several sections labeled "Construct Validity," "Concurrent Validity," and the like. One does not have to be thoroughly versed in the different aspects of validity to get enough information about the extent of validity evidence for the instrument. (The interested reader can find a discussion of the meaning of the different aspects of validity in the "Additional Considerations" section below.)

The modern view of validity, in fact, is that the different "types" of validity are actually aspects of a single concept—construct validity. Construct validity indicates what meaning can be attached to the scores from an instrument. Rather than examining the several, often overlapping types of validity, one should focus on the main inferences that underlie the use of an instrument. And by *use* we mean both the use for which it was intended and the use you plan to make of it. The typical assumptions underlying the use of instruments for management development are, as indicated above, that the instrument is measuring what it says it measures, that scores are related to effectiveness, and that the constructs measured are amenable to change.

Look in the validity section of the technical materials for studies that compare scores on the instrument to scores on another validated instrument (that is, an instrument whose psychometric properties are known). Favorable results in this type of study will provide some evidence that the instrument measures what it was intended to measure. Another kind of study to look for would be one that tests hypotheses about observable behaviors. For example, the instrument developer may hypothesize that certain scales on the instrument will be related to certain personality characteristics. Other types of studies that can test this assumption are described below in the "Construct Validity" section.

The next underlying assumption to be tested is that scores on the instrument are related to important aspects of managerial effectiveness on the job. The typical way to test this hypothesis is to compare scores on the instrument to some other data relating to effectiveness or competence. These data, if collected at the same time as the ratings on the instrument, reflect current effectiveness. Raters may be asked to rate the target manager on a different effectiveness measure; current performance-appraisal data may be collected; or data may be obtained that relate to current employee or work-group productivity. In addition, effectiveness data or data on promotions may be collected after some time has elapsed, so that we can know whether performance can be predicted by scores on the instrument from an earlier time.

Look for any information about studies that relate scores on the instrument to another measure of effectiveness on the job. This other measure could be another instrument that has been completed on the manager, or it could be a rating on effectiveness done by the manager's boss or co-workers. In a correlational study, look for correlations that are at least moderate in magnitude (.3 or higher). Or look for a study that has compared instrument scores for groups of managers considered to be performing effectively or ineffectively—high performers or low performers. In this case, look for a result that shows that scores on the instrument were able to predict membership in the high and low groups (that is, scores of managers in the high group were greater than scores of managers in the low group).

The third type of study to look for is one that shows that the concepts measured are amenable to change as a result of training, feedback, or other developmental experiences. This is the most difficult study to find, because very few instrument developers have done this research. Studies of change resulting from feedback are very scarce.

One additional issue in examining validity is the sample used in any of the studies. How well do the characteristics of the sample reflect those of your target population? If the sample was primarily white males and your target audience will be more diverse, check to see whether gender or ethnic differences were found in the research on the instrument in question.

If you plan to use an instrument internationally, issues to be concerned with include the quality of translation, the availability of international norms, and evidence of reliability and validity for international samples.

Translating an instrument should be a carefully executed, multistage process, including both translation from English to the other language, as well as independent translation from the other language back into English. The use of back-translation ensures that meaning has not been changed in the process. Careful attention should be paid to idioms during this process. For example, "putting out fires" is common jargon among North American managers but has a different, more literal interpretation in both the nonmanagement arena and in areas outside the United States.

It is not always the case that an instrument translated for international use includes translated feedback and development materials. Many instrument vendors have translated only the instrument itself but not the feedback report or development guide. Products such as this can be used for English-speaking managers whose raters are not fluent in English. They cannot, however, be used for managers who themselves are not fluent in English because they will be unable to read their feedback. Thus, if your target managers do not speak English, check thoroughly the completeness of translation for all materials related to the instrument.

Finally, instruments developed from research, theory, or experience with North American managers must undergo further testing with the population for whom the instrument will be used. At a minimum, norms should be available for each language in which the instrument is translated. To compare North American managers' scores to scores of managers from other cultures, look for statistical evidence supporting score equivalence. This would include factor analyses, scale alphas, and mean comparisons for each intended population. Vendors who have substantial databases should have statistical evidence, such as differential item functioning (DIF), item response theory (see, for example, Ellis, 1989), and logistic regression (LR) (see, for example,

Swaminathan & Rogers, 1990) supporting the equivalence of the questions. Also, cross-cultural validity studies should be undertaken to verify that scores on the instrument are related to effectiveness in the other cultures.

The pace at which instrument publishers are translating instruments for international users has increased, and it is not uncommon to find instruments that have been translated into more than one language. It is, however, difficult to find North American-developed instruments that have been validated for the population for which they're translated.

So a cautious approach is warranted when selecting North American-developed instruments for non-English-speaking managers. Look for one that has been carefully translated and which has been studied with respect to cross-cultural differences in norms, factor structure or scale reliabilities across different groups, and whether scores are related to effectiveness in similar ways across different cultures.

Keep in mind, however, that no instrument is ever proven valid once and for all. Validity is an ongoing process that involves collecting evidence over time in varying situations for different populations. In fact, any time the intended use of an instrument departs significantly from the assumptions underlying validity research to date, more research needs to be done.

It is useful to think of validity as a continuum ranging from no evidence that the inferences underlying the instrument are valid, to some evidence, to a good deal of evidence among varying groups and in different contexts. In general, the number of validity studies done should correspond roughly to how long the instrument has been around. Newer instruments will have fewer studies reported, but all instruments that offer feedback from co-workers should have at least one study completed that indicates the instrument is measuring what it claims to measure, and one that shows that its scores are related to effectiveness.

Additional Considerations: Ways of Defining Validity

According to psychometricians and statisticians, there are several aspects of validity: construct, concurrent, predictive, and content.

Construct Validity. A construct is an abstract variable that cannot be directly measured. Temperature and humidity are not constructs; but leadership, resourcefulness, and integrity are.

Construct validity refers to the ability of the instrument to measure phenomena that are hypothesized to exist but for which we can have no direct measure. All the different "types" of validity (content, concurrent, predictive) are actually aspects of construct validity. Every validity study represents a test of hypotheses about relationships between a set of constructs. Some constructs are narrow, in the sense that they may be completely described by a few behaviors. Other constructs are so large or broad that they may never be perfectly defined by even a very large number of behaviors. Broad constructs, like leadership, are usually measured using only a subset of all possible behaviors.

Thinking about construct validity begins with thinking about the theory, if any, that has been used to specify the meaning of the construct; how the construct should be related to other constructs; and how it should be related to specific observable behaviors. One way construct validation research can proceed is by testing hypotheses generated about observable behaviors. Another strategy may be to compare scores on the target instrument to scores on a similar instrument whose psychometric properties are known.

Because constructs cannot be directly measured, another way to approach construct validity is through a multimethod study. For example, if we are measuring more than one construct (resourcefulness and integrity) and can measure them in multiple ways (paper-and-pencil and rater observations), then we can discern how much of the correlation between these two constructs is due to the measurement method and how much is due to overlap in the constructs themselves. To obtain evidence of construct validity in our example, the correlation between the paper-and-pencil and rater observation measures of resourcefulness should be greater than the correlation between resourcefulness and integrity using the same measurement technique. *Convergent validity* is the label given to the condition of a high correlation between the same construct measured by two different methods.

Concurrent and Predictive Validity. These two aspects of validity, known collectively as criterion-related validity, have to do with the relationship of the scores to some other attribute, called a criterion variable. With 360-degree-feedback instruments, we are usually concerned with criteria that measure managerial performance or effectiveness.

Both concurrent and predictive validity are temporal in nature. Concurrent validity has to do with the relationship between scores on an instrument and performance or effectiveness measured at approximately the same time the instrument was completed. The relevant question is: How accurate is the instrument's assessment of current performance or effectiveness? Predictive validity has to do with the relationship between scores on the instrument and performance or effectiveness sometime in the future. (Though some people use the term *predictive* to cover any study that looks at the relationship with effectiveness, we will limit our use of this term to mean only those studies that relate current scores to future performance.) The relevant question here is: How accurately can the instrument predict future performance or effectiveness?

Both concurrent and predictive studies are relevant for instruments used for management development, because in helping managers become more effective we are interested in both current effectiveness and effectiveness over the long term.

Criterion issue. In studies of both these types, the nature and measurement of the criterion variable is a key issue. Examining the criterion measure employed to validate an instrument can be as important as examining the study's findings.

Remember that all leadership and management instruments are intended to assess factors associated with success or effectiveness. But success can be thought of as upward movement in one's career (that is, promotion in the organization), or it can be thought of in terms of effectiveness as a leader or manager (that is, how satisfied others are with the individual's performance, how well the manager's direct reports perform, measures of profit-and-loss, and the like). These two phenomena are not necessarily the same (Luthans, 1988). Understanding how success has been defined in the research on an instrument and knowing how that compares with your own intended use of it is key to interpreting the results of any validity study.

According to Dalton (1996), the main, and only really appropriate, use of data from a 360-degree-feedback instrument is for management development or assessment for development. Most instruments of this type have not been developed or extensively tested for other uses (for example, selection or promotion). These instruments are basically dealing with people's perceptions of behavior or competence, rather than any completely objective measure of performance (if one exists). An individual or organization planning to use an instrument of this sort for selection, promotion, pay, or performance purposes is in treacherous territory and will need to become aware of the relevant professional standards (SIOP, 1987) and government guidelines (Mohrman, Resnick-West, & Lawler, 1990), which are not covered in this report.

For management development, the main inferences to be drawn are that (1) high scores are related to effective current performance and (2) the competencies represent areas managers are able to develop.

Finding an appropriate criterion for a study of the first inference would involve choosing a definition of effective performance: If it is defined as the boss's perception of the individual's performance, the criterion variable might be performance-appraisal data; if it is defined by direct reports' perceptions, the criterion might be "effectiveness" as rated by direct reports; and if it is defined as success in the organization, the criterion might be promotions.

Variables less directly related to managerial effectiveness, such as bottom-line business profitability, may not be the best criterion measures. Businesses can be profitable for reasons other than good management, and businesses can fail despite good management.

A useful study of the second inference would show that managers are able to improve their scores as a result of training, feedback, or other developmental efforts on their part. As mentioned earlier, this type of study is more difficult to find.

Choosing the criterion variable for a validity study is one of the more problematic but critical phases of the research. The choice should be made with reference to the main inference(s) to be drawn from the instrument scores. In general, criterion data from an independent source (that is, a source different from the person or persons providing ratings on the instrument) are usually considered better data because using an independent source reduces the bias that occurs when both pieces of data come from the same person.

Reliability of criterion measure. A good criterion measure should have a high degree of reliability. In other words, whatever it measures should be constant over time. When effectiveness ratings are used as the criterion measures, they are subject to some of the same reliability concerns as the instrument itself. For example, raters' judgments about the overall effectiveness of their leaders may be unstable over short periods of time. Although this issue is an important one to think about in evaluating the quality of a validity study, it may be difficult to find such research because few instrument developers have taken the time to study the reliability of their criterion measures.

Content Validity. Content validity has to do with the degree to which the items are a representative and comprehensive measure of the phenomenon in question, in this case leadership or management skills. For example, a 360-degree-feedback instrument should cover areas that are important for effective performance for the job in question. Often this information can be derived from the theory or model on which the instrument was developed, or from the experience of the instrument developer. Content validity is often more a matter of professional judgment than statistical analysis.

There Is No Perfect Instrument: Balance Is the Key

Remember throughout this process that there is no perfect instrument—no one instrument that is perfect for everyone, no one instrument that will always be ideal for you, and no one instrument that can't be improved. As solid and powerful as some are, each feedback tool has its weaknesses as well as its strengths.

The key to good instrument selection is balance—knowing what you need and seeking a balance between your needs and quality standards. You may have already made some conscious trade-offs, and before this selection process ends you may make some more—sacrificing one good to get another. But to maximize the value of your choice—to most effectively use the instrument you choose—you need to be aware of the trade-offs you have made— what you have lost and what you have gained.

Keep in mind that no instrument is proven valid once and for all. Validation is an ongoing process. Several good validity studies defining effectiveness in varying ways are stronger than a single study or several studies that define effectiveness in the same way.

Now that you have reviewed the origin of items and feedback scales and have examined the evidence of reliability and validity for the instruments, you have available one or more instruments that you believe have been constructed according to sound psychometric principles. At this point you can begin to evaluate and compare instruments in terms of their potential impact—what kind of feedback will be provided and how that will be delivered.

STEP 9:
THINK ABOUT FACE VALIDITY

Go to the instrument itself—the items to which the manager will respond. Read through the items carefully. Experiment with them by trying to apply them to a manager whose skills you can observe in your organization. Do the items make sense when applied to someone you know? If you go through this exercise with several different managers in mind, you will get a sense of how managers who complete the instrument will feel about its face validity. Face validity isn't validity in the technical sense but rather whether the instrument looks appropriate for your managers. If the items are awkward or hard to apply, think about dropping this instrument from consideration.

STEP 10:
EXAMINE THE RESPONSE SCALE

Look at the main response scale—the choices people will have when they respond to each item. Examining this helps you understand how people will be asked to think about the competencies measured by the instrument.

Will they be asked to rate the competencies as either "Strengths" or "Areas for development" or will they be asked to make finer distinctions in rating levels of skill?

Response scales (also called rating scales) usually range from 2 points to 10 points. Both shorter and longer scales have their advantages as well as their disadvantages. A 2-point scale will force one to choose between alternatives such as "Yes/No," "Strength/Development needed," or "Do more/Do less." The advantage of the shorter scale is simplicity of feedback.

The trade-off with a shorter scale is in data richness. With a short response scale, raters will not be able to report middle levels of competency and may fail to respond to items if they are unwilling to say definitely "Yes" or "No," definitely "Strength" or "Development needed." And short scales are not useful if one intends to use a pre- and post-test design to look at the impact of feedback or training, because these can fail to pick up the subtle changes fostered by even the best training or change efforts. If any follow-up studies will be conducted down the road, an instrument with a longer response scale will be needed.

A longer scale (5 to 7 points) will allow raters to make finer distinctions. The trade-off with a longer scale may be some ambiguity in the meaning of what may be too many response categories. Choosing between "Occasionally" and "Sometimes" may be difficult on some items or for some managers. Some examples of longer scales include:

Never	Very uncharacteristic	Among the best
Occasionally	Uncharacteristic	Better than most
Sometimes	Slightly uncharacteristic	Average
Usually	Slightly characteristic	Worse than most
Always	Characteristic	Among the worst
	Very characteristic	

As can be seen in the three examples above, some response scales give raters a middle-of-the-road choice, such as "Average," whereas others force raters to take at least a slightly positive or slightly negative position.

In addition, a response scale may have "Don't know" or "Not applicable" alternative choices. These may be useful if you are using the instrument for a combined population of managers and nonmanagers—or with people new to their positions—and want people to have these rating options. The downside is that raters may overuse the "Don't know" option to avoid making difficult rating choices.

STEP 11:
EVALUATE THE FEEDBACK DISPLAY

Type of Display

There are two types of feedback display: graphic and narrative. Many feedback displays use a combination of styles to present data.

Graphic displays are charts or graphs that provide a visual picture of how managers view themselves in comparison to their raters and the instrument norms.

Narrative display is computer-generated feedback in text format rather than graphic format. It is both a presentation and a personalized interpretation of the scored data, as opposed to boilerplate recommendations for change. The text produced often incorporates some of the same strategies for framing feedback as can be found in graphic displays (see the section below [Step 13] on strategies for facilitating interpretation and change).

Narrative interpretation differs from development materials (discussed on pages 28-29) in that narrative is personalized, based on the manager's individual feedback and output as a result of the scoring process. Development materials are off-the-shelf manuals, workbooks, and readings.

Clarity of Feedback Display

Open and review the sample feedback as if it were your own. It is probably best not to use your own feedback (if you've already taken the instrument) in this step, because your feelings about your own results may impede an objective analysis.

Carefully read through the instructions and look at the display. Can you understand it? How easy is this for you? Your own experience in trying to interpret the feedback is a good measure of how others will experience it. If it takes you several attempts to understand the graphic display, it is probably too complicated.

Although people should ideally never be handed instrument feedback without some guidance, it is not always possible to provide large groups of managers with intensive support. In general, the more interpretation and goal-setting that managers will have to do for themselves, the more you should be concerned about the clarity of the feedback display.

STEP 12:
UNDERSTAND HOW BREAKOUT OF RATER RESPONSES IS HANDLED

By *rater responses,* we mean the responses that come from the people who rated the manager. This usually includes direct reports, peers, boss(es), and customers. Find out how rater data are treated in the feedback display.

Most 360-degree-feedback instruments present boss, peer, direct report, and customer ratings as separate average scores, but some combine the ratings of all "others" into one average score. Other instruments display the average rating from direct reports separately but combine boss ratings with peers.

Using separate ratings for each rater group may be more powerful, in that it gives the manager more information. It can also be more complicated to interpret, more compromising of rater anonymity, and more painful to receive. Again, consider how much guidance and support you, or others in your organization, will be providing managers when they receive their feedback. The more guidance people receive, the better they are able to benefit from the enhanced impact that feedback from separate rater groups can provide.

An issue with providing separate boss feedback is that rater confidentiality is compromised. If only one supervisor completes the instrument on a manager, his or her responses will be exposed under the "boss" category. Even if supervisors have been made aware (as they should be) that their responses will be known to the manager, confidentiality is still an issue to consider.

Raters who know or believe that their responses will not be confidential may not be completely open in their evaluations, compromising the quality of their data. Although breakout of rater data increases impact, it may decrease confidentiality and, occasionally, data quality. However, we believe that because the various rater groups often have very different perspectives of a manager's performance, it is better to present the ratings from each perspective separately.

Step 13:
Learn What Strategies Are Used to Facilitate Interpretation of Scores

Enhancing performance or changing behavior is difficult, even when feedback on these areas has been comprehensive. The difficulty is partly because the feedback can be overwhelming, especially if there is a lot of it, if it is negative, or if it comes from many different perspectives. Without some map or guidance about what is most important to direct one's attention to, the recipient can get lost, miss important data, or give up on processing the information.

Rather than just presenting self and rater scores, an instrument should build some kind of framework for corrective action into the feedback display.

There are at least seven strategies for helping managers understand their feedback:

- comparison to norms,
- highlighting largest self-rater discrepancies,
- item-level feedback,
- highlighting high/low scores,
- comparison to ideal,
- importance to job or success, and
- "Do more/Do less" feedback.

These can be built into either graphic or narrative displays.

Any feedback display should use at least one of these strategies because without any of them, the manager has no way of knowing what to make of his or her scores. The better feedback displays usually use a combination of two or more strategies.

If well-laid out and clearly integrated, the use of multiple strategies may increase the meaningfulness as well as the impact of the data. This is because it will give the manager many viewpoints from which to examine the information and make it more difficult for the recipient to dispute negative feedback. Yet, past a point, more may not be better. For some managers, more information may be too much, especially if the display is comprehensive but not entirely clear. Again, it is up to you to decide whether the balance between information/impact and clarity/simplicity is right for your target group.

Comparison to Norms

Comparison to norms is probably the most widely used of all strategies. Norms usually represent an average for all people who have taken the instrument but sometimes are based on one specific target group (middle managers, for example). These averages are presented for each scale on which feedback is received so that the manager can compare his or her own scores to the norm. The manager uses this information to ask himself or herself: How am I doing compared to others? The more the norm group resembles the manager in terms of managerial level, the more relevant this comparison will be.

Norms can be displayed in a variety of ways. They can be listed as a separate column of data to be compared visually to one's own score, or one's own score can be plotted against norm data. When this latter strategy is used, the graphic display contains standard scores or percentiles. A standard score is a statistical computation that allows individual scores to be compared to the total distribution of scores by taking into account the mean and standard deviation of the population. A percentile represents the percentage of persons who have lower scores than the individual being rated.

Norms for diverse populations (for example, gender, industry, country) are usually located in the trainer's manual. How often a vendor updates norms will depend on assumptions about the theory behind the instrument. If skills and abilities measured by an instrument are believed to be sensitive to changes over time, then norms should be updated on a regular basis. When this is the case, skills do not disappear from effective managers' repertoire, but instead the relative importance of them changes with trends in organizations. For example, managers today are more aware of the importance of teamwork as organizations have become flatter in their structure. If, on the other hand, there is no reason to believe that the importance of skills and abilities will fluctuate over time and if there is statistical evidence to support this, then cumulative norms or norms that include everyone who has taken the instrument are sufficient. Newly developed instruments and instruments that have recently been translated will most likely use cumulative norms because only a small number of managers have taken the instrument.

Highlighting Largest Self-rater Differences

Although by definition all 360-degree-feedback instruments present self-ratings compared to others' ratings, some feedback displays go beyond these comparisons to highlight scores on scales where self-rater discrepancies are meaningful. Managers often wonder how much of a difference between ratings is enough to be meaningful, and this type of highlighting lets them know. It can be very useful, especially when combined with rater breakout of data. For example, the ratings of self and peers on scales that concern managing people may be similar, whereas the ratings of direct reports may be significantly lower than self-ratings. This can happen because supervisory skills are often most visible to those being supervised.

Item-level Feedback

Though item-level feedback can be unreliable (that is, single items do not adequately represent complex phenomena), it can be helpful when used in conjunction with feedback on scales because items provide more detailed information. Learning that you scored low on "Resourcefulness," for example, may not be as helpful as knowing how you scored on the specific items linked to "Resourcefulness." Item-level feedback can give the manager some leads about what to begin to do differently in order to be more effective.

Highlighting High/Low Scores

High and low scores are sometimes presented on individual items and sometimes on scales. This type data can be presented as graphs or as listings with symbols to denote the highest and lowest scores.

Highlighting the high and low scores can provide participants with a quick overview of their strengths and weaknesses, especially when they are receiving a lot of feedback. The danger is that when high and low scores are item scores, what is presented can be a smattering of items from many different scales—which may be an unreliable summary of the data. The more useful approach may be to present high and low scale scores, with representative high or low items highlighted within scales.

Comparison to Ideal

Comparison to an ideal is not widely used. When used, it may represent a theoretical ideal for leadership or management, or it may be data provided by the manager himself or herself (for example, What kind of leader do I see as ideal?) or by raters (for example, What kind of leader do raters see as ideal?). Self or rater data on actual performance can then be compared to data from self or raters on the ideal leader.

Importance to Job or Success

Importance ratings may reflect perceptions of how important a skill or practice is to effectiveness in one's job or to longer-term success in one's organization. These data are usually collected from managers and/or from their raters when the instrument is completed. Sometimes raters rate each item or scale in terms of its importance (to the job or to success), and sometimes they choose a certain number of items and scales that are most important.

The use of this strategy can be very powerful in prioritizing which parts of the feedback may need greatest attention, especially when the manager and his or her boss agree. Managers who are rated low on several scales can check the importance data and focus their developmental efforts on areas that were seen as important for their short-term or longer-term effectiveness. When the manager and boss do not agree, importance data can provide a fairly non-threatening way to begin a conversation about the overall results.

Some caution should be used, however, in working with ratings of importance to job or success. Importance ratings may reflect people's impressions of what has gotten executives to the top as much as real and critical leadership competencies. These ratings may vary depending on the perspective of the person providing the data (the manager's boss, peers, or direct reports). Mid-level managers may rate importance for success differently than executives. And ratings may change over time with changes in organizational culture or business strategy. In addition, few instrument developers who provide this type feedback have assessed the reliability of importance ratings.

"Do More/Do Less" Feedback

"Do more/Do less" feedback is not used by many instruments but can be a valuable piece of information, especially when respondents are allowed to rate how frequently a behavior or practice is observed. "Monitoring the progress of direct reports' work" is a good example. A high score would mean the manager monitors work frequently, or does a lot of monitoring. What the manager cannot know from this is whether it is good to do a lot of monitoring or whether he or she is doing the appropriate amount. Although norms will tell the manager how he or she is doing relative to other managers, they will not shed light on whether direct reports are satisfied with this level of behavior. Asking raters to indicate whether managers should do more or do less provides an opportunity to see their side of the picture.

Linking Strategies Together: Issues in Considering Impact of Feedback

Different combinations of feedback strategies will produce different kinds of impact on the manager receiving the feedback and may result in different conclusions being drawn from the data. Consider the blend of strategies presented in the feedback design, what that blend will highlight for managers, and what the impact will be. Again, maximum impact may not always be desired. The goal should be meaningful feedback with appropriate impact.

If you still have several possible choices once you've gotten to this point in the selection process, it may be worthwhile to take these instruments yourself, have them scored, and receive your own feedback. This kind of experience is especially important if you have any doubts about the impact the feedback will have or whether the depth of intervention will be appropriate. A second-best alternative is to fill one out, as an exercise for yourself only, on someone else. As you complete the questionnaire itself, consider the feel or nature of the items. Sometimes items which look just fine become unclear or awkward when you actually have to use them to rate a real person.

If you do have the opportunity to review your own feedback, pay attention to your own reactions to the competencies being measured by the scales, how rater data are broken out, and what graphic strategies are used in the feedback display to help managers understand and interpret their scores.

STEP 14:
LOOK FOR DEVELOPMENT AND SUPPORT MATERIALS

Support for the Manager's Development

At this point in the process, having considered potential impact, you are now ready to consider what support will be available with each instrument for both the manager receiving feedback and the trainer or facilitator responsible for one-on-one consultation or classroom training.

During a feedback process, managers should be carefully led through the graphic presentation of their scores where they learn something about their strengths and development needs. Yet they may remain unaware of what these scores mean. They may have an answer to the question, "What are my strengths and weaknesses as a leader?" but may lack answers to, "So what does that mean?" and "Now what should I do?" With feedback instruments, the "So what?" question can be addressed by development materials and the "Now what?" question by a goal-planning process. These kinds of support materials accompany the feedback packet with some instruments but are not a part of some others.

Instruments can have exquisite accompanying materials ranging from nicely bound development guides for managers (including in-depth interpretive materials, suggestions for development, and goal-planning guides), to notebooks, manuals, overhead materials, extra norm data, and group profile options for trainers. Some instruments, however, offer very little besides the feedback.

We have intentionally left what an instrument offers in this regard as one of the last steps in our evaluation process. It would be a mistake to select an instrument because of its glitzy package without considering the integrity of its development and the quality of its feedback display. Once you know you've gotten the best instrument for you in those two arenas, you may want to choose the one with the best accompanying materials.

And, with supporting materials, quantity is not necessarily the same as quality. More is not necessarily better. For example, for most audiences, it is best to look for materials that help managers come up with solutions and goals of their own, because people are more motivated to implement their own ideas than to do what they have been told. Yet some development guides are very prescriptive. They have a "Do A, B, and C" approach to development. And some materials appear to be presented in a boilerplate fashion. Sophisticated managers may lose faith in an instrument that appears to give everyone the same advice.

Trainer Support

To evaluate support for the trainer, what is available must be compared to your own needs as a trainer or facilitator (or the needs of those who will be responsible for feedback facilitation). Some instruments come with training guides that give a more in-depth understanding of how to interpret scores on the instrument. Find out if attendance in a certification workshop is required for purchase and use. Supplemental norms may be available, either in the form of organizational norms or norms on unique subsamples (for example, health-care workers, cross-cultural groups, student leaders, high-level executives, and so forth). Videotapes may be available for classroom use, as might other additional materials including transparencies, handouts, or supplemental technical reports.

Scoring Process

Computer scoring is the most common method of producing feedback. Computer scoring can be done by the vendor; licensed scoring programs; or self-administered, self-scoring computer software. Some instruments have manually scored (hand-scored) versions available as well.

Computer Scoring

In general, although all computer scoring tends to increase the total price to the consumer, this method has many benefits. The depth and quality of computer-generated feedback tends to be high. Instead of the manager sifting through mounds of data to find, for example, the ten highest rated items, the computer program can sort and arrange the information in a fraction of the time. Human errors in scoring the data and calculating scale scores can be eliminated by using computer scoring. It also can provide raters with greater anonymity and can enhance the quality of their responses because they know the target managers will not see their rating forms. Computer scoring can be done by the vendor or software can be purchased from the vendor.

Vendor Scoring. Returning instruments to the source where they were purchased is a very common form of instrument scoring. It does, of course, increase the cost per instrument, as well as introduce the issue of turnaround time (the time it takes to mail forms or fax forms to the vendor, have those scored, and have feedback reports produced and returned to the client). Though there may be some problems, many managers and trainers find vendor scoring to be the most expedient method because it can reduce managers' and trainers' time by relieving them of the job of hand-scoring the instruments. It also tends to produce some of the highest quality feedback in a visual sense.

Some vendors license their scoring programs to clients. Initial costs of the license can be high, but for organizations that purchase large quantities of instruments, this method can be cost effective.

Licensed scoring arrangements will vary according to the clients' needs and work environment. Organizations may be able to purchase software to score instruments on-site or may be able to use both on-site scoring and vendor assistance through remote scoring (using a modem to send data to the vendor to score). Computer programs for mainframes also can sometimes be purchased through the vendor. If your organization has the appropriate equipment (for example, modem, fax machine, optical scanner, personal computer, and printer) and the resources to support these systems, this scoring method can provide quick turnaround of high-quality reports for those who process a large number of instruments.

Computer Software. Instruments that are sold for use with personal computers usually have scoring programs built into the software. The quality of the feedback can be as good as any other computer-scored instrument. This method can, however, have a benefit over other computer-scoring methods, in that the software can be reused over time.

Each of these scoring methods has its advantages and disadvantages. Time, costs, equipment, frequency of use, quantity and quality of feedback, and confidentiality are all issues that require your consideration before deciding which method best suits your organizational needs.

Manual Scoring

Hand-scored instruments allow managers to compile their own data and produce their own feedback. This scoring method gives managers a firsthand knowledge of how scores are calculated and plotted, and it allows for immediate turnaround of feedback to the manager.

Although hand-scoring has these benefits, its strengths can easily become its weaknesses. Asking inexperienced users to score their own instruments increases the likelihood of error and invalid results.

Assuring rater confidentiality is another difficulty with hand-scored instruments. Some instruments require managers to transfer raters' scores onto summary sheets. It can be possible for managers to guess who each rater might be from the number of respondents, their handwriting, or the pattern of responses. Such a compromise of confidentiality can damage the quality of the data by reducing the frankness of the raters' evaluations. In cases where rater confidentiality is of a particular concern, a person not involved in the rating process can be chosen to hand-score instruments.

STEP 15:
COMPARE COST—VALUE FOR THE PRICE

Cost is always a consideration, but what is included in the price can vary so extensively that selecting an instrument based solely on cost can result in a less than optimal instrument for your use.

To adequately conduct the feedback process for one manager, you would need one self-report instrument, at least three instruments for raters (usually the minimum to have rater data scored), a development guide, and an arrangement for scoring. Sometimes the cost includes all these and sometimes it includes only single copies of the instrument. Certification workshops, organizational profiles, trainers' guides, introductory videos, and post-assessment may all be available but at additional cost. It takes thorough investigation to determine what is included in the quoted price and what supplemental services may be available at additional cost.

STEP 16:
CONSIDER LENGTH A MINOR ISSUE

Time is often a factor when choosing between one instrument with a few and another instrument with a large number of questions. Some managers may find an instrument that requires 45 minutes to an hour to complete a bothersome task and may reject its use. Though a longer instrument may require more initial completion time, the depth of feedback it produces may be worth the initial investment.

Conclusion

Congratulations! You have completed the selection process and now have one or more carefully developed and well-designed feedback instruments for possible use in your organization.

You probably have made some compromises along the way. Be aware of what those are and think through their implications. Doing this may help you make the final choice if you are left with more than one possible instrument. You may also want to contact vendors again for any additional information that can help you choose between instruments or aid in the understanding or use of your instrument of choice. And remember to remain aware of the implications of any trade-offs you have made.

References

American Psychological Association (APA). (1985). *Standards for educational and psychological testing*. Washington, DC: Author.

Conoley, J. C., & Impara, J. C. (Eds.). (1995). *Mental measurements yearbook.* The Buros Institute of Mental Measurements (12th ed.). Lincoln, NE: The University of Nebraska.

Dalton, M. (1996). Multirater feedback and conditions for change. *Consulting Psychology Journal: Practice and Research, 48,* 12-16.

Ellis, B. B. (1989). Differential item functioning: Implications for test translations. *Journal of Applied Psychology, 74*(6), 912-921.

Hogan, J., & Hogan, R. (1990). *Business and industry testing: Current practices and test reviews.* Austin, TX: Pro-Ed.

Krug, S. E. (1993). *Psychware sourcebook.* Champaign, IL: Metritech, Inc.

Luthans, F. (1988). Successful vs. effective real managers. *The Academy of Management Executive, 2,* 127-132.

Mohrman, A., Resnick-West, S., & Lawler, E. (1990). *Designing performance appraisal systems.* San Francisco: Jossey-Bass.

Society for Industrial and Organizational Psychology (SIOP). (1987). *Principles for the validation and use of selection procedures.* College Park, MD: Author.

Swaminathan, H., & Rogers, H. J. (1990). Detecting differential item functioning using logistic regression procedures. *Journal of Education and Measurement, 27,* 361-370.

Sweetland, R., & Keyser, D. J. (Eds.). (1990). *Tests: A comprehensive reference for assessment in psychology, education and business* (3rd ed.). Austin, TX: Pro-Ed.

Van Velsor, E., & Leslie, J. (1991). *Feedback to managers, volume II: A review and comparison of sixteen multi-rater feedback instruments.* Greensboro, NC: Center for Creative Leadership.

Suggested Readings

American Psychological Association (APA). (1993). *Responsible test use: Case studies for assessing human behavior*. Washington, DC: Author.

Anastasi, A. (1988). *Psychological testing* (6th ed.). New York: McMillan.

Bracken, D. (1994, September). Straight talk about multirater feedback. *Training and Development*, pp. 44-51.

Clark, K., & Clark, M. (Eds.). (1990). *Measures of leadership*. West Orange, NJ: Leadership Library of America.

Ghiselli, E., Campbell, J., & Zedeck, S. (1981). *Measurement theory for the behavioral sciences*. San Francisco: W. H. Freeman.

Hollenbeck, G., Dalton, M., Pollman, V., Bracken, D., Jako, R., & McCauley, D. (in press). *Forum: Should 360-degree feedback be used for administrative as well as development purposes?* Greensboro, NC: Center for Creative Leadership.

Jones, J., & Bearley, W. (1996). *360-degree feedback: Strategies, tactics, and techniques for developing leaders*. Amherst, MA: HRD Press.

Lyman, H. (1986). *Test scores and what they mean* (4th ed.). Englewood Cliffs, NJ: Prentice Hall.

Nowack, K. (1993, January). 360-degree feedback: The whole story. *Training and Development*, pp. 69-72.

Peters, D. (1985). *Directory of human resource development instrumentation*. San Diego, CA: University Associates.

Prince, J. M., & Fleenor, J. W. (in press). *Using 360-degree feedback in organizations: An annotated bibliography*. Greensboro, NC: Center for Creative Leadership.

Tornow, W. W., London, M., & Associates. (in press). *Maximizing the value of 360-degree feedback: A process for individual and organizational development*. San Francisco: Jossey-Bass.

Yukl, G. (1995, December). How to get the most out of 360-degree feedback. *Training, 32*, 45-50.

Zeidner, M., & Most, R. (Eds.). (1992). *Psychological testing: An inside view*. Palo Alto, CA: Daves-Black.

Glossary of Terms

Behavioral item—A word, phrase, or sentence that describes some aspect of behavior.

Cluster analysis—A statistical analysis that groups like objects or items.

Concurrent validity—The relationship between scores on an instrument and performance or effectiveness measured at about the same time the instrument was completed.

Construct—An abstract variable that cannot be directly measured.

Construct validity—The ability of the instrument to measure phenomena that are hypothesized to exist but for which we can have no direct measure.

Content validity—The degree to which the items are a representative and a comprehensive measure of the phenomenon in question.

Correlation coefficient—A number, resulting from statistical analysis, that indicates the strength of a relationship between two measures.

Criterion variable—A behavior or phenomenon separate from, but presumably related to, ratings produced by the instrument.

Cronbach's alpha—A measure of the internal consistency of scales, based on the average correlation among items and the number of items; if this coefficient is low, either the scale contains too few items or the items have little in common.

Differential item functioning (DIF)—A statistical analysis that tests equivalence of an instrument for two populations that have equal abilities.

Empirical—Capable of being demonstrated or verified by scientific (usually statistical) methods.

Face validity—Whether the instrument looks like it measures what it is intended to measure.

Factor analysis—A set of statistical approaches to grouping items or variables into categories known as factors.

Feedback—Information about a person's performance or behavior, or the impact of performance or behavior, that is intentionally delivered to that person in order to facilitate change or improvement.

Feedback display—The presentation of scored data, represented graphically or in narrative form.

Graphic display—Charts or graphs that provide a visual numeric portrayal of data.

Halo effect—High correlations resulting from raters' overall bias toward the individual.

Hypothesis—An expectation or prediction about observable phenomena derived from theory.

Independent criteria—A criterion variable that comes from a different source or is external to the instrument itself.

Internal consistency—The average correlation among items included on the same scale.

Internally homogeneous—Having high internal consistency.

Interrater reliability—Agreement among ratings within rater groups.

Item—A word, phrase, or sentence that describes an aspect of behavior, performance, skill, or personal characteristic.

Item content—The behavior, skill, or characteristic to which an item refers.

Item level—Referring to each item individually.

Item response theory (IRT)—A statistical analysis that tests whether members of different populations (for example, English and French), who are assumed to be "matched" on the abilities measured by an instrument, answer the questions in a similar fashion. Examinees are matched using the item score patterns.

Item-scale correlations—The relationship(s) between responses to individual items and computed scores on scales.

Logistic regression (LR)—A statistical analysis that tests the equivalence of an instrument for two populations by using the total instrument score (or a score adjusted by deleting questionable items) to match examinees.

Mean—Arithmetic average of a set of data points or numbers.

Model—A set of hypotheses about the relationships between variables or constructs.

Multimethod study—A study that compares the correlation between two constructs measured by different methods (for example, rater observation and paper-and-pencil methods). The correlation between the two different constructs measured similarly should be lower than that between a single construct measured using different methods.

Narrative display—Data presented in text format, usually with personalized interpretation.

Norm group—Group of managers whose scores are stored in the vendor's test database and are output as a comparison on every individual feedback report.

Norms—The average scores of all people who have taken the instrument or the average scores of specific target groups.

Population—The whole universe or group from which samples are drawn.

Predictive validity—The relationship between scores on an instrument and performance or effectiveness measured at a future time.

Psychometrics—The study or practice of statistically measuring aspects of performance, behavior, personal characteristics, and other human attributes.

Rater groups—Groups of individuals providing responses to items on an instrument.

Raters—Individuals providing responses on an instrument.

Rational/intuitive scale development—Grouping items together based on the authors' expectations or experience about how different skills or behaviors relate to one another.

Response scale—A set of response choices provided on an instrument for raters to use in evaluating behavior, performance, or skill.

Sample—A subset of individuals drawn from the total population or database.

Scale—A group of items that have logical and empirical coherence.

Standard deviation—A statistical index indicating the amount of spread in the distribution of scores around the average score of a sample.

Statistical scale development—Using statistical-grouping procedures such as factor analysis, cluster analysis, or item-scale correlations to sort items into scales based on the degree of similarity in the response patterns of raters.

Target population—A group, sometimes with particular characteristics, for whom the instrument is intended; the group that will be rated on an instrument.

Test-retest reliability—Stability of scores over short periods of time.

Validation strategy—The process or set of studies used to collect evidence regarding the uses to which scores from an instrument can be reasonably and meaningfully applied.

Validity—The extent to which an instrument measures what it is supposed to measure; the appropriateness of the inferences made about scores from an instrument.

Variable—Any measurable entity whose value is not constant or given.

Weighting—Assigning differential value to points on a scale.

Instrument Evaluation Checklist

GETTING STARTED

(1)   Find out what is available.

Have you done a thorough search for management or leadership development instruments? Check the source book(s) you've examined.

_____ *Feedback to Managers, Volume II*

_____ *Business and Industry Testing: Current Practices and Test Reviews*

_____ *Mental Measurements Yearbook*

_____ *Tests: A Comprehensive Reference for Assessment in Psychology, Education and Business*

_____ *Psychware Sourcebook*

_____ promotional brochures from instrument publishers

_____ other sources

(2)   Collect a complete set of materials.

Do you have all of the following for each instrument being reviewed?

_____ a copy of the instrument

_____ a sample feedback report

_____ a technical manual

_____ supporting materials (sample development guide, list of trainer materials, etc.)

_____ purchasing information (price, scoring, certification, etc.)

(3)   Compare your intended use to instrument characteristics. What are
the special needs, job demands, etc., of your target managers?

List below any competencies important to your organization or in the
program in which the instrument will be used.

_____

_____

_____

_____

_____

_____

_____

_____

Has the instrument been normed on a sample similar to your target
managers, in terms of level, gender, ethnicity, etc.?

_____ Yes   _____ No

(4)   Examine the feedback scales.

Are the instrument's scales a good fit with your organization's or
training program's management or leadership model?

_____ Yes   _____ No   _____ Maybe

Are the instrument's scales a good fit with your target audience (level
and role of employees/managers who will get feedback)?

_____ Yes   _____ No   _____ Maybe

CHECKPOINT: ELIMINATE NOW THOSE INSTRUMENTS NOT MEET-
ING YOUR NEEDS IN TERMS OF TARGET AUDIENCE OR DOMAINS
(FEEDBACK SCALES).

(5)   Familiarize yourself with instrument-development process.

(6)   Learn how items and feedback scales were developed.

What is the source of the instrument's items? (more than one may apply)

_____ theory

_____ research

_____ experience

What is the nature of item content? (more than one may apply)

_____ behavioral

_____ skill-based

_____ trait or characteristic-based

What types of statistical methods were used for scale development?

_____ factor analysis

_____ cluster analysis

_____ item-scale correlations

(7)   Find out how consistent scores tend to be.

Internal consistency

_____ scales have coefficients between .6 and .8

Interrater agreement

_____ scales have coefficients between .4 and .7

Test-retest

_____ scales have coefficients greater than .4

(8) Assess basic aspects of validity—does the instrument measure what it claims to measure? (Look in technical manual.)

Found at least one study showing instrument measures what it says it measures (for example, comparing scores on this instrument to hypotheses about scores or to scores on another instrument)?

_____ Yes   _____ No

Found at least one study showing scores on the instrument are related to a measure of effectiveness?

_____ Yes   _____ No

The sample used in research studies reflects characteristics of your target audience?

_____ Yes   _____ No

If instrument will be used internationally:

Has it been translated and back-translated?

_____ Yes   _____ No

_____ Instrument itself

_____ Feedback report

_____ Development materials

Are international norms available?

_____ Yes   _____ No

Have reliability and validity been studied internationally?

_____ Yes   _____ No

CHECKPOINT: ELIMINATE NOW THOSE INSTRUMENTS HAVING LITTLE EVIDENCE OF RELIABILITY OR VALIDITY.

CONSIDER POTENTIAL IMPACT

(9)   Think about face validity.

Is item wording clear, manager-oriented, and absent of gender or ethnic bias?

_____ Yes   _____ No

(10) Examine the response scale.

Does the length meet your needs?

_____ Yes   _____ No

Is there a nonresponse option (that is, "Don't know," "Not applicable")?

_____ Yes   _____ No

(11) Evaluate the feedback display.

What type of display is used in the feedback?

_____ Graphic

_____ Narrative

Is the display understandable?

_____ Clear and understandable (understood almost immediately)

_____ Somewhat difficult to interpret (took two to three attempts to understand)

_____ Very hard to understand (still had trouble after three attempts)

(12) Understand how breakout of rater responses is handled. (More than one category may apply.)

_____ Feedback from boss shown separately

_____ Feedback from peers shown separately

_____ Feedback from direct reports shown separately

_____ No breakout of rater data (all of the above categories combined)

(13) Learn what strategies are used to facilitate interpretation of scores.

_____ Comparison to norms

_____ Highlighting largest self-rater discrepancies

_____ Item-level feedback

_____ Highlighting high/low scores

_____ Comparison to ideal

_____ Importance to job or success

_____ "Do more/Do less" feedback

CHECKPOINT: AT THIS TIME, ELIMINATE THOSE INSTRUMENTS WITH ITEMS THAT DO NOT MAKE SENSE OR ARE INAPPROPRI-ATE, HAVE RESPONSE SCALES THAT DO NOT MEET YOUR NEEDS (IN TERMS OF LENGTH OR NONRESPONSE OPTIONS), OR HAVE STRATEGIES FOR INTERPRETING SCORES THAT ARE DIFFICULT TO USE OR UNDERSTAND.

(14) Look for development and support materials.

Is there support for the manager's development?

_____ Development guide

_____ Goal-planning worksheets

_____ Workshop available

_____ Vendor hotline

Is there trainer support?

_____ Trainer's manual

_____ Workshop available

_____ Overheads

_____ Video

_____ Supplemental norms available

Is certification required?

_____ Yes   _____ No

How is scoring done?

_____ Manually scored

_____ Computer-scored

_____ Vendor-scored

_____ Computer software

OTHER CONSIDERATIONS

(15) Compare cost—value for the price.

Does the price of the instrument compare favorably to others and is it within the range you can afford?

_____ Yes   _____ No

(16) Consider length a minor issue.

Is the instrument either excessively long or too brief to be useful and acceptable for your managers?

_____ Yes   _____ No

CENTER FOR CREATIVE LEADERSHIP
New Releases, Best-sellers, Bibliographies, and Special Packages

NEW RELEASES

IDEAS INTO ACTION GUIDEBOOKS

Ongoing Feedback: How to Get It, How to Use It Kirkland & Manoogian (1998, Stock #400) .... $6.95 *

Reaching Your Development Goals McCauley & Martineau (1998, Stock #401) .... $6.95 *

Becoming a More Versatile Learner Dalton (1998, Stock #402) .... $6.95 *

Giving Feedback to Subordinates Buron & McDonald-Mann (1999, Stock #403) $6.95

Choosing Executives: A Research Report on the Peak Selection Simulation Deal, Sessa, & Taylor
(1999, Stock #183) $20.00

Coaching for Action: A Report on Long-term Advising in a Program Context Guthrie (1999,
Stock #181) $20.00

The Complete Inklings: Columns on Leadership and Creativity Campbell (1999, Stock #343) $30.00

Geographically Dispersed Teams: An Annotated Bibliography (Sessa, Hansen, Prestridge, &
Kossler (1999, Stock #346) $20.00

High-Performance Work Organizations: Definitions, Practices, and an Annotated Bibliography
Kirkman, Lowe, & Young (1999, Stock #342) $20.00

Internalizing Strengths: An Overlooked Way of Overcoming Weaknesses in Managers Kaplan
(1999, Stock #182) $15.00

Positive Turbulence: Developing Climates for Creativity, Innovation, and Renewal
Gryskiewicz (1999, Stock #2031) $32.95

Selecting International Executives: A Suggested Framework and Annotated Bibliography
London & Sessa (1999, Stock #345) $20.00

Spirit and Leadership Moxley (1999, Stock #2035) $30.95

Workforce Reductions: An Annotated Bibliography Hickok (1999, Stock #344) $20.00

BEST-SELLERS

The Adventures of Team Fantastic: A Practical Guide for Team Leaders and Members Hallam
(1996, Stock #172) $20.00

Breaking Free: A Prescription for Personal and Organizational Change Noer (1997, Stock #271) $25.00

Breaking the Glass Ceiling: Can Women Reach the Top of America's Largest Corporations?
(Updated Edition) Morrison, White, & Van Velsor (1992, Stock #236A) $13.00

The Center for Creative Leadership Handbook of Leadership Development McCauley, Moxley,
& Van Velsor (Eds.) (1998, Stock #201) .... $65.00 *

CEO Selection: A Street-smart Review Hollenbeck (1994, Stock #164) ....$25.00 *

Choosing 360: A Guide to Evaluating Multi-rater Feedback Instruments for Management
Development Van Velsor, Leslie, & Fleenor (1997, Stock #334) .... $15.00 *

A Cross-National Comparison of Effective Leadership and Teamwork: Toward a Global
Workforce Leslie & Van Velsor (1998, Stock #177) $15.00

Eighty-eight Assignments for Development in Place Lombardo & Eichinger (1989, Stock #136) .... $15.00 *

Enhancing 360-degree Feedback for Senior Executives: How to Maximize the Benefits and
Minimize the Risks Kaplan & Palus (1994, Stock #160) .... $15.00 *

Evolving Leaders: A Model for Promoting Leadership Development in Programs Palus & Drath
(1995, Stock #165) .... $15.00 *

Executive Selection: A Look at What We Know and What We Need to Know DeVries (1993,
Stock #321) .... $20.00 *

Executive Selection: A Research Report on What Works and What Doesn't Sessa, Kaiser,
Taylor, & Campbell (1998, Stock #179) .... $30.00 *

Feedback to Managers (3rd Edition) Leslie & Fleenor (1998, Stock #178) .... $60.00 *

Four Essential Ways that Coaching Can Help Executives Witherspoon & White (1997, Stock #175) $10.00

A Glass Ceiling Survey: Benchmarking Barriers and Practices Morrison, Schreiber, & Price
(1995, Stock #161) $15.00

High Flyers: Developing the Next Generation of Leaders McCall (1997, Stock #293) $27.95

How to Design an Effective System for Developing Managers and Executives Dalton &
Hollenbeck (1996, Stock #158) .... $15.00 *

If I'm In Charge Here, Why Is Everybody Laughing? Campbell (1984, Stock #205) .... $9.95 *

If You Don't Know Where You're Going You'll Probably End Up Somewhere Else Campbell (1974, Stock #203) .... $9.95 *

International Success: Selecting, Developing, and Supporting Expatriate Managers Wilson & Dalton (1998, Stock #180) .... $15.00 *

Leadership Education: A Source Book of Courses and Programs Schwartz, Freeman, & Axtman (Eds.) (1998, Stock #339) .... $40.00 *

Leadership Resources: A Guide to Training and Development Tools Schwartz, Freeman, & Axtman (Eds.) (1998, Stock #340) .... $40.00 *

The Lessons of Experience: How Successful Executives Develop on the Job McCall, Lombardo, & Morrison (1988, Stock #211) $27.50

A Look at Derailment Today: North America and Europe Leslie & Van Velsor (1996, Stock #169) .... $20.00 *

Making Common Sense: Leadership as Meaning-making in a Community of Practice Drath & Palus (1994, Stock #156) .... $15.00 *

Making Diversity Happen: Controversies and Solutions Morrison, Ruderman, & Hughes-James (1993, Stock #320) $20.00

Managerial Promotion: The Dynamics for Men and Women Ruderman, Ohlott, & Kram (1996, Stock #170) $15.00

Managing Across Cultures: A Learning Framework Wilson, Hoppe, & Sayles (1996, Stock #173) $15.00

Maximizing the Value of 360-degree Feedback Tornow, London, & CCL Associates (1998, Stock #295) .... $42.95 *

The New Leaders: Guidelines on Leadership Diversity in America Morrison (1992, Stock #238A) $18.50

Perspectives on Dialogue: Making Talk Developmental for Individuals and Organizations Dixon (1996, Stock #168) .... $20.00 *

Preventing Derailment: What To Do Before It's Too Late Lombardo & Eichinger (1989, Stock #138) $25.00

The Realities of Management Promotion Ruderman & Ohlott (1994, Stock #157) .... $15.00 *

Selected Research on Work Team Diversity Ruderman, Hughes-James, & Jackson (Eds.) (1996, Stock #326) $24.95

Should 360-degree Feedback Be Used Only for Developmental Purposes? Bracken, Dalton, Jako, McCauley, Pollman, with Preface by Hollenbeck (1997, Stock #335) .... $15.00 *

Take the Road to Creativity and Get Off Your Dead End Campbell (1977, Stock #204) .... $9.95 *

Twenty-two Ways to Develop Leadership in Staff Managers Eichinger & Lombardo (1990, Stock #144) $15.00

BIBLIOGRAPHIES

Formal Mentoring Programs in Organizations: An Annotated Bibliography Douglas (1997, Stock #332) $20.00

Management Development through Job Experiences: An Annotated Bibliography McCauley & Brutus (1998, Stock #337) $20.00

Selection at the Top: An Annotated Bibliography Sessa & Campbell (1997, Stock #333) .... $20.00 *

Succession Planning: An Annotated Bibliography Eastman (1995, Stock #324) .... $20.00 *

Using 360-degree Feedback in Organizations: An Annotated Bibliography Fleenor & Prince (1997, Stock #338) .... $15.00 *

SPECIAL PACKAGES

Executive Selection (Stock #710C; includes 157, 164, 179, 180, 321, 333) $85.00

Guidebook Package (Stock #721; includes 400, 401, 402) $14.95

HR Professional's Info Pack (Stock #717C; includes 136, 158, 169, 201, 324, 334, 340) $100.00

Leadership Education and Leadership Resources Package (Stock #722; includes 339, 340) $70.00

New Understanding of Leadership (Stock #718; includes 156, 165, 168) $40.00

Personal Growth, Taking Charge, and Enhancing Creativity (Stock #231; includes 203, 204, 205) ... $20.00

The 360 Collection (Stock #720C; includes 160, 178, 295, 334, 335, 338) $75.00

Discounts are available. Please write for a Resources catalog. Address your request to: Publication, Center for Creative Leadership, P.O. Box 26300, Greensboro, NC 27438-6300, 336-286-4480, or fax to 336-282-3284. Purchase your publications from our on-line bookstore at **www.ccl.org/ publications**. All prices subject to change.

*Indicates publication is also part of a package.

ORDER FORM

Or e-mail your order via the Center's on-line bookstore at www.ccl.org

Name _____ Title _____

Organization _____

Mailing Address _____
(street address required for mailing)

City/State/Zip _____

Telephone _____ FAX _____
(telephone number required for UPS mailing)

Quantity	Stock No.	Title	Unit Cost	Amount

CCL's Federal ID Number
is 237-07-9591.

Subtotal	
Shipping and Handling (add 6% of subtotal with a $4.00 minimum; add 40% on all international shipping)	
NC residents add 6% sales tax; CA residents add 7.75% sales tax; CO residents add 6.1% sales tax	
TOTAL	

METHOD OF PAYMENT
(ALL orders for less than $100 must be PREPAID.)

❏ Check or money order enclosed (payable to Center for Creative Leadership).

❏ Purchase Order No. _____ (Must be accompanied by this form.)

❏ Charge my order, plus shipping, to my credit card:
      ❏ American Express ❏ Discover ❏ MasterCard ❏ VISA

ACCOUNT NUMBER:_____ EXPIRATION DATE: MO.___ YR.___

NAME OF ISSUING BANK: _____

SIGNATURE _____

❏ Please put me on your mailing list.

Publication • Center for Creative Leadership • P.O. Box 26300
Greensboro, NC 27438-6300
336-286-4480 • FAX 336-282-3284

Client Priority Code: R

fold here

CENTER FOR CREATIVE LEADERSHIP
PUBLICATION
P.O. Box 26300
Greensboro, NC 27438-6300